Cheshire in Camera

Victorian and Edwardian Photographs of Cheshire

by
Frederick Woods

Shiva Publishing Limited

SHIVA PUBLISHING LIMITED
4 Church Lane, Nantwich, Cheshire CW5 5RQ

© Frederick Woods, 1983

ISBN 0 906812 58 5

Typeset and printed by Devon Print Group, Exeter

Cheshire in Camera

Introduction

Change and decay in all around I see. There are, of course, those who would not agree with the hymnist H.F. Lyte, and who would maintain that change equals progress and is therefore automatically beneficial. In certain aspects of life this is doubtless true; I doubt whether anyone would wish to return to some of the living conditions of our forebears, to their relative lack of medical facilities, their gross inequality of opportunity. But in many other respects it is difficult to put one's hand on one's heart and swear that all change is for the best. It is not merely our surroundings that have changed, it is the quality of life itself; tranquillity and spaciousness have fled for ever, it seems. And if the Industrial Revolution was the beginning of the deterioration, 1914 was the point at which that slide steepened vertiginously and irreversibly.

This collection of photographs is a reminder of what Cheshire used to be like before that climacteric, in the days of Victoria and Edward VII. It is a record of long-demolished buildings (victims of apathy or that dread and rampant disease *avaritia culti*), obliterated landscapes and extinct businesses. Nostalgia will always be a potent part of the older generations' outlook, and I hope that this book will revive pleasant memories. To younger generations it will, I trust, be both a kind of gentle education and a stimulus to resist, in their own era, developers who are more concerned with personal profit than the community environment.

FW, 1983

Acknowledgements

I must acknowledge with gratitude the permission to reprint some of these photographs, given by:

The Libraries and Museums Department of Cheshire County Council; Tameside Local Studies Library; the Trustees of the Nantwich Museum; Walls Meat Co.; Mr H. Bentley; Mr M. Clarke; Mrs G. Jackson; Mr B. Key; Mrs D.M. Kyle; Mrs A. Lloyd; Mr C. Ray; Miss M. Redfern; Mr B. Smith; Mrs R.J. Whalley; Mr D. Whitfield; Mrs L. Williams.

The picturesque Artists Lane in Alderley Edge, 1904.

Cars and buildings now cover this tranquil spot—The Cross at Alderley Edge in 1909.

Station Road, Alsager, 1905.

Railway Street, Altrincham, 1909, with cab rank and horse-trough at the tram terminus.

A packed horse-bus makes its leisurely way down Stamford New Road, Altrincham, 1907.

The Old Bank, Altrincham, ca 1905.

A family group on a cycling jaunt, outside Astbury Church during the summer of 1900.

Audlem's main street in 1909, showing subtle architectural differences but a world away in terms of atmosphere.

A long-forgotten feeling of spaciousness at Woodside, Birkenhead, 1904.

A cobbled and relaxed Charing Cross in Birkenhead, 1904.

An unattended horse attracts little attention as it ambles up Palmerston Street, Bollington, one fine day in 1907.

The unspoiled village of Burton at the turn of the century.

These relaxed gentlemen, believe it or not, are celebrating the end of a timed bicycle race from Manchester to Calveley. L to R: Messrs Colley, Higham, Cummings and Butler. The photograph was taken at the Davenport Arms, ca 1914, and Mr Cummings looks remarkably cool, considering the clothes he apparently raced in!

SCHOOLS HILL, CHEADLE.

Schools Hill, Cheadle, ca 1905.

The archaeological dig for Roman remains in Chester during 1863, when the hypocaust was uncovered.

The old public market and Guildhall in Chester ca *1905.*

A rather quiet market day in Chester during the early years of this century, beneath a flag that seems undecided whether it is at half-mast or not.

Eastgate, looking in towards the city centre, ca 1903.

A day at Chester races ca *1906.*

Chester Mills and weir during the 1890s, with the City Floating Baths at the left.

Chester Castle and Dee Bridge, 1903.

Eccleston Ferry, Chester, ca 1908.

Congleton High Street, 1906.

The cab rank outside Crewe Station, ca 1900. The corner of the Crewe Arms Hotel is just visible on the right.

The Market Square, Crewe, in 1906, showing railway-built houses in Market Street. A horse-bus is on its way from the station to Merrill's Bridge.

Hillock Farm, Victoria Street, Crewe. The house had to be demolished in 1926 when it was damaged by earth tremors.

Crewe's bonfire for the Coronation of Edward VII in 1902. It was 35 yards wide, 70 feet high and weighed 250 tons.

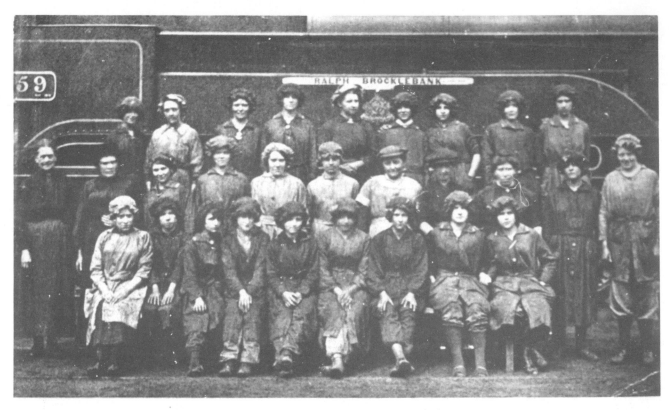

The beginning of the end for Crewe Works. In 1915, against intense Union opposition, women were brought in to work on the railway to replace enlisted men. They were made to do the 'dirty' jobs as well as the clean, presumably to make sure they would not want to stay on after the war.

An uprooted garden shed being assessed at the old Toll House, Dukinfield, 1902.

The oddly foreign-looking Dukinfield Lodge in its Victorian heyday, ca 1890.

MANCHESTER SHIP CANAL, EASTHAM.

The Manchester Ship Canal at Eastham, ca 1904.

Contrasting modes of transport at Gatley outside the Horse and Farrier, which also marked the tram terminus, 1903.

A desolate but tranquil view of Werneth Low, Gee Cross, at the beginning of this century.

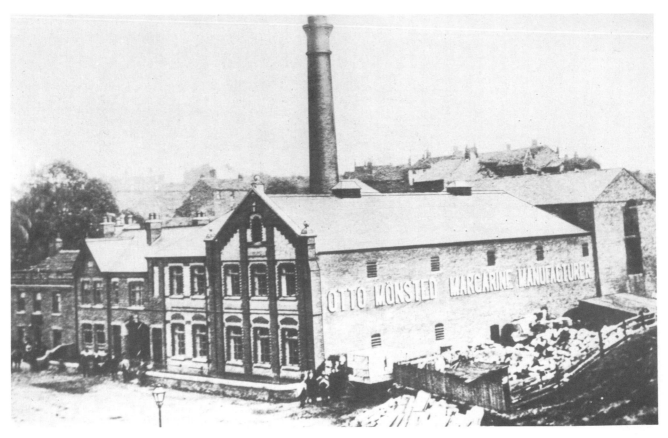

Otto Mönsted's margarine factory, once a dominating feature of Godley Hill, photographed in 1912. The site is now occupied by an even bigger Walls Meat factory.

The centre of Harthill village at the turn of the century, with the old school on the left and Raw Head looming behind.

The deserted village of Havannah, near Congleton, once a thriving mill town. After the mill failed, the place became a ghost town and remained so for several decades. The row of houses on the left in this photograph, ca 1905, are now demolished and a factory stands in their place, but those on the right are once again inhabited. The mill at the end of the street is in ruins.

THE VILLAGE HESWALL.

Most of the village of Heswall as it was in 1906, a tranquil scene spoiled only by the excessively ugly telegraph pole.

The square at Holmes Chapel, taken in early 1910.

The peaceful Market Street in Hoylake, as it was some time in the early part of this century.

Hoylake Promenade and beach, 1911.

Apprehensive-looking local inhabitants in Mill Lane, Haughton Green, Hyde, ca 1903. The factory chimney probably belonged to Kingston Mill.

The old corn mill at Hyde, photographed in 1884.

Market Place, Hyde, ca 1900. Note the now-rare sight of horse-droppings in the road!

Wood End Lane in Hyde, about 1907.

King Street, Knutsford, showing The Rose and Crown (built 1647) before its characterless reconstruction in 1925.

A view of Knutsford from the railway line, ca 1907. The area in front and to the right of the church is now largely car park.

Bridgewater Street, Lymm, as it was in 1907.

A busy day in the Market Place at Macclesfield in the summer of 1908. The Boots sign reaches across the years to us.

By way of contrast, Macclesfield's Chestergate on a very quiet day in 1905. The cash stationers
seems to be selling an enormous range of goods, including gas, clocks and Wills Imperial Salt.

Looking down Church Street, Malpas, during the early 1900s.

The Cross, Malpas.

The Cross at Malpas in 1909.

The old bridge at Marple, 1905.

An old toll-house, set in a quiet country lane at Marple, 1907.

An elderly sufferer in a bath-chair is drawn by an apparently equally elderly helper towards restoration at the Railway Inn at Meols, 1912.

Evidently a popular meeting-place for young people—the Bull Ring at Middlewich, ca 1908.

The Deep Cutting, Mottram, photographed from the Stalybridge side. The cutting was completed in 1826.

A view of the cluttered but cosy-looking Spout Green, Mottram, taken in 1907.

Donkey-cart and carefully-positioned attendants at The Stocks, Mottram Old Road, one summer's day in 1890.

The Market Square, Nantwich, as it was before 1868, when the pillared Market Hall was demolished.

Hightown, Nantwich, in 1880. Oatmarket is on the right.

Garnet's Corner at the top of Hospital Street, Nantwich, during the 1890s.

The Temperance Commercial Hotel, Nantwich, during the 1860s. The railed-in grave belonged to the Foster family, owners of Shrewbridge Hall, which afterwards became the Brine Baths Hotel. The stone now lies under the central tree in the churchyard.

A rare picture of the Crown Hotel, Nantwich, plastered from head to foot and with separate windows on the top floor. This tasteless alteration was carried out by N. Piggott (an ancestor of Lester Piggott) and the building was restored to its original state by his successor. This photograph dates from the turn of the century.

The first steam-driven bus leaves Nantwich for Crewe, July 1905.

The Square, Nantwich

The Square, Nantwich, 1907.

An emulation that didn't last, though the New Brighton Tower dominated the Wirral coastline during its lifetime. This photograph was taken in 1904.

A view up Victoria Road, New Brighton, taken from the pier in the early years of this century.

Two houses in Warrington Road, Northwich, which were originally level with the road. They were victims of the wide-spread subsidence caused by salt-working, and an example of more conventional subsidence can be seen at the extreme right of the photograph, which is dated 1903.

The Angel Hotel in the Bull Ring, Northwich, 1911.

The old salt-works at Northwich, 1903. Not a pretty sight!

High Street and the Bull Ring, Northwich, 1904.

A butcher's shop in Runcorn during the first ten years of this century—and a striking testimony to the lack of air pollution in those days.

Halton Castle, Runcorn, seen from across the unspoilt fields, 1908.

The Black Bear, Sandbach, looking the worse for wear and with a remarkably humped roof, taken about 1898.

The crowded Market Place in Sandbach, 1905.

'The Pride of Cheshire', a showman's engine made by Fodens, complete with six fairground trailers. Photographed ca 1890 on London Road, Sandbach, with Elworth Vicarage (now demolished) behind.

A crowd of crazed sensation-seekers gathers round the corpse of a tram that has gone off the rails at Stalybridge, ca 1904.

Grosvenor Square, Stalybridge, as it was in 1905.

Emmett's Portrait Gallery and the Stalybridge Cotton Famine Relief Office in Melbourne Street, 1863.

A lonely smithy, The Brushes, Stalybridge, 1897.

Looking like a child's toy, a train crosses the Mersey by Stockport Viaduct, ca 1910.

The then sylvan Didsbury Road, at Heaton Norris, Stockport, in 1907.

Lockwood Fold, at Stockport, at the beginning of the century.

Not greatly different from now but a lot more peaceful: High Street, Tarporley in 1907.

The Horse Fair at Warrington in the early years of this century. Hiring fairs and horse fairs largely died out after the First World War.

Bridge Street, Warrington, ca 1907.

The Widnes Transporter, which carried the courageous below an unbroken span of 1000 feet over the Mersey. This photograph was taken prior to 1906, when the design of the transporter was changed; it was finally demolished in 1963.

Chapel Lane, Wilmslow, as it was at the turn of the century.

Rush-hour in Winsford High Street, around 1903.

Huntsman's Bridge, just outside Winsford, photographed in 1910. The bridge, no longer standing, presumably marked the boundary between two properties, hence the gate at its centre.

A scene redolent of more spacious days, photographed at The Flashes, Winsford, in 1912.

And, by way of contrast, the bustling port of Winsford on the River Weaver, 1910.

Making lump salt the hard way, Winsford, 1904.

A quiet country lane led up to Wistaston church in the old days. This photograph dates from the first five years of the century.

Wybunbury as it was in 1908, looking away from the west door of the church.

WYBUNBURY.

Wybunbury church and, in the background, the Swan, taken at about the same time as the preceding picture.

Other titles of interest

Legends and Traditions of Cheshire
Frederick Woods

Further Legends and Traditions of Cheshire
Frederick Woods

The Great Fire of Nantwich
Jeremy Lake